The Hum

by **Rachel Sparks**

and **Penny Coltman**

Contents

Outside our bodies **2**
Making faces **3**
How did you begin? **4**
A breath of fresh air **6**
All about blood **8**
The food journey **10**
Waterworks **11**
Check up on teeth **12**
Get to know your skeleton **14**
On the move **15**
The body's control centre **16**
Feeling hot, feeling cold **17**
Eye spy **18**
Feeling in touch **20**
Smells good! **21**
Tasty information **22**
Can you hear me? **23**
Spot the senses **24**
A healthy menu **26**
Work, rest and play **28**
What about drugs? **29**
Our amazing bodies **30**
Glossary of words used in this book **31**
Index **32**

Outside our bodies

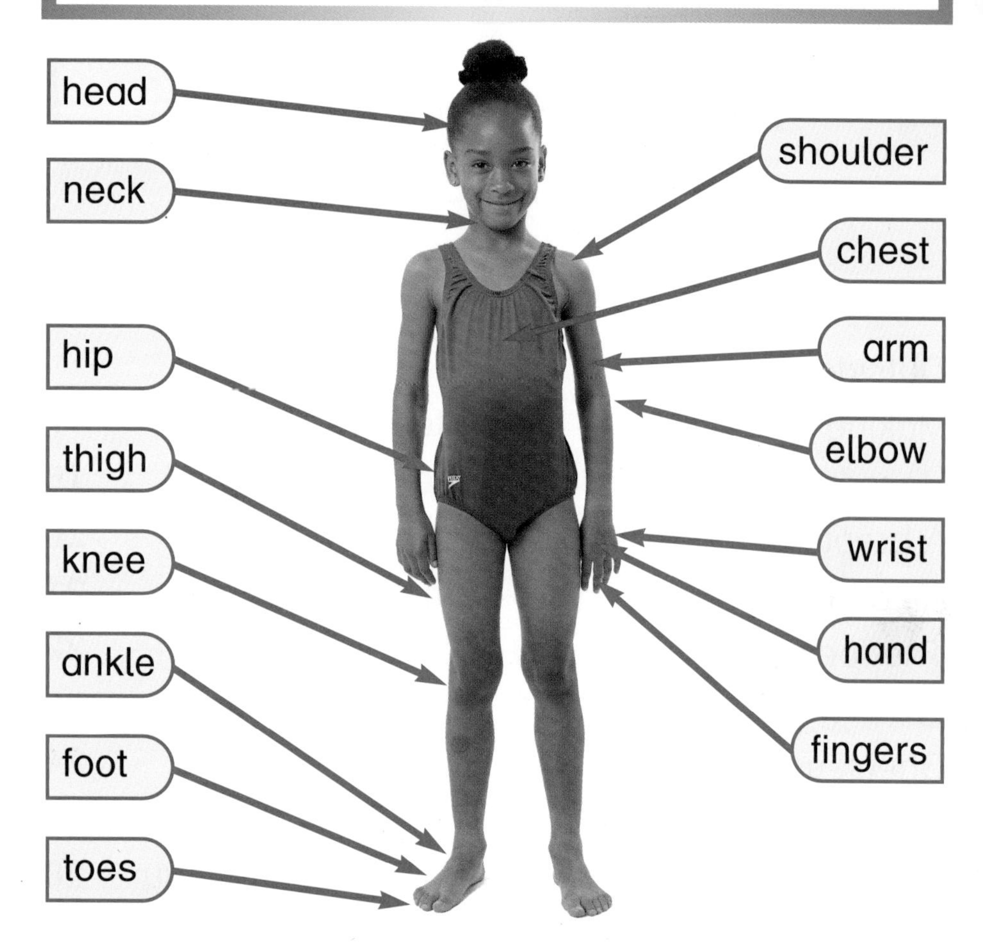

The outside of our bodies is covered in skin. Skin is able to stretch as we grow. All the time, new skin is made as outside layers are worn away. Skin protects the delicate insides of our bodies.

Making faces

We can move our faces in complicated ways because of many tiny muscles. Expressions are an important way of showing others how we feel.

What happens to your face when you are sad?

surprised

Be happy! Scowling uses more muscles than smiling.

happy

angry

How did you begin?

A baby takes about nine months to develop in its mother's womb.

This time line shows the changes which take place during these months. All this happened before you were born!

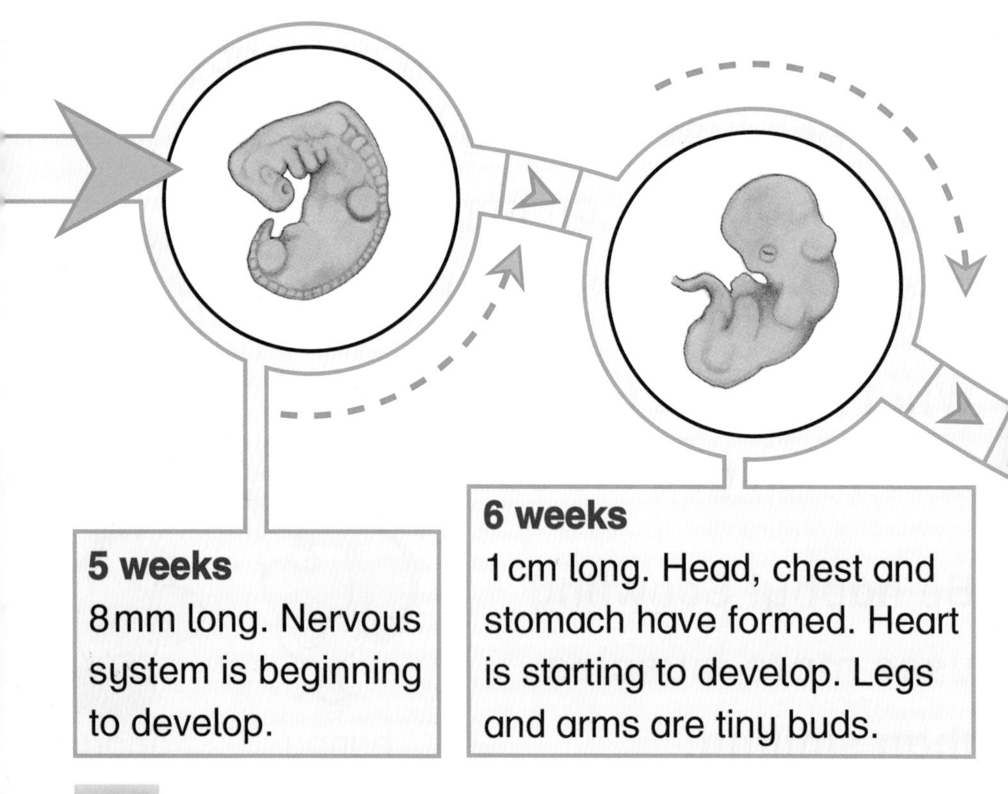

5 weeks
8 mm long. Nervous system is beginning to develop.

6 weeks
1 cm long. Head, chest and stomach have formed. Heart is starting to develop. Legs and arms are tiny buds.

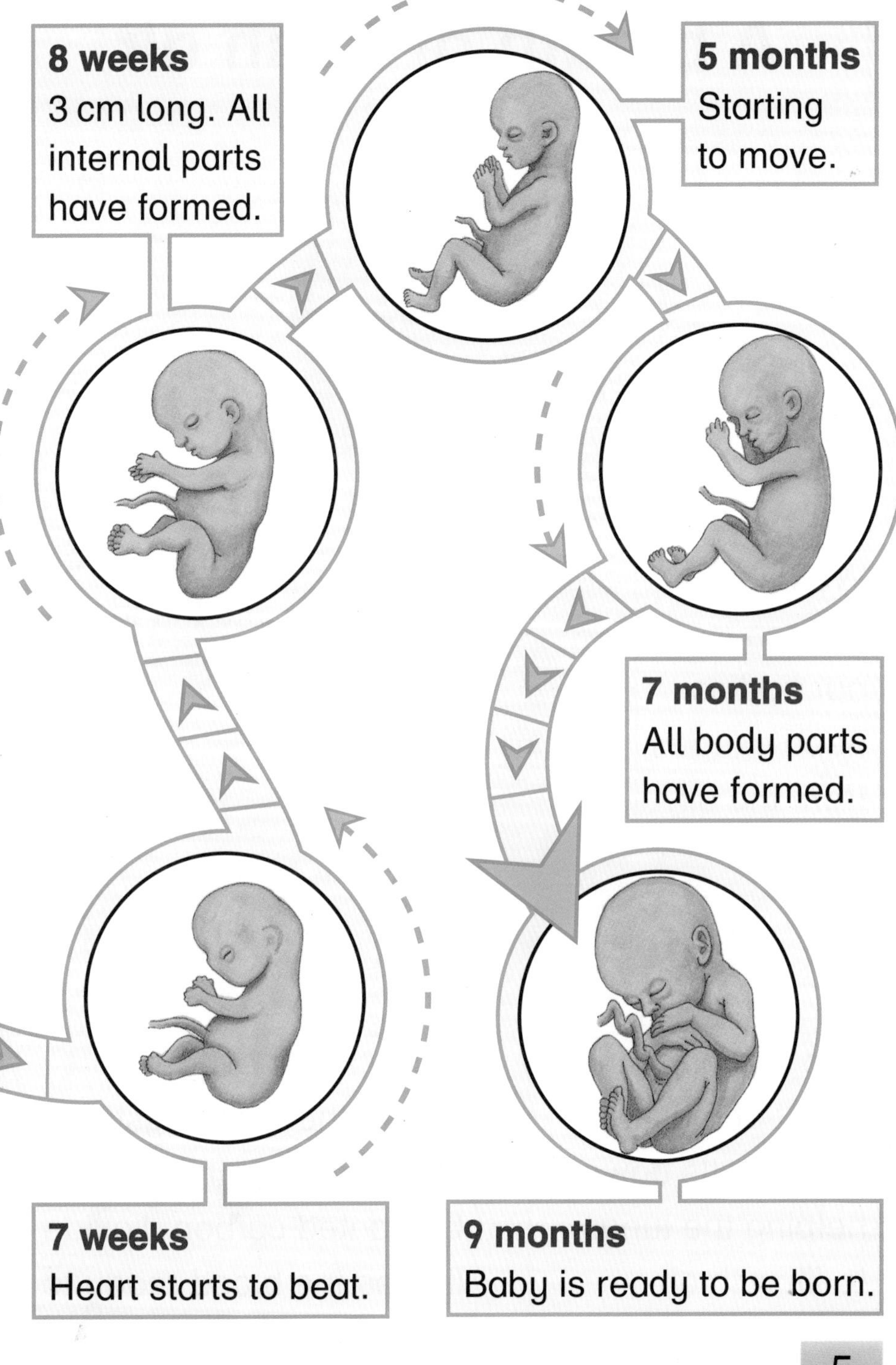
8 weeks
3 cm long. All internal parts have formed.
5 months
Starting to move.
7 months
All body parts have formed.
7 weeks
Heart starts to beat.
9 months
Baby is ready to be born.

A breath of fresh air

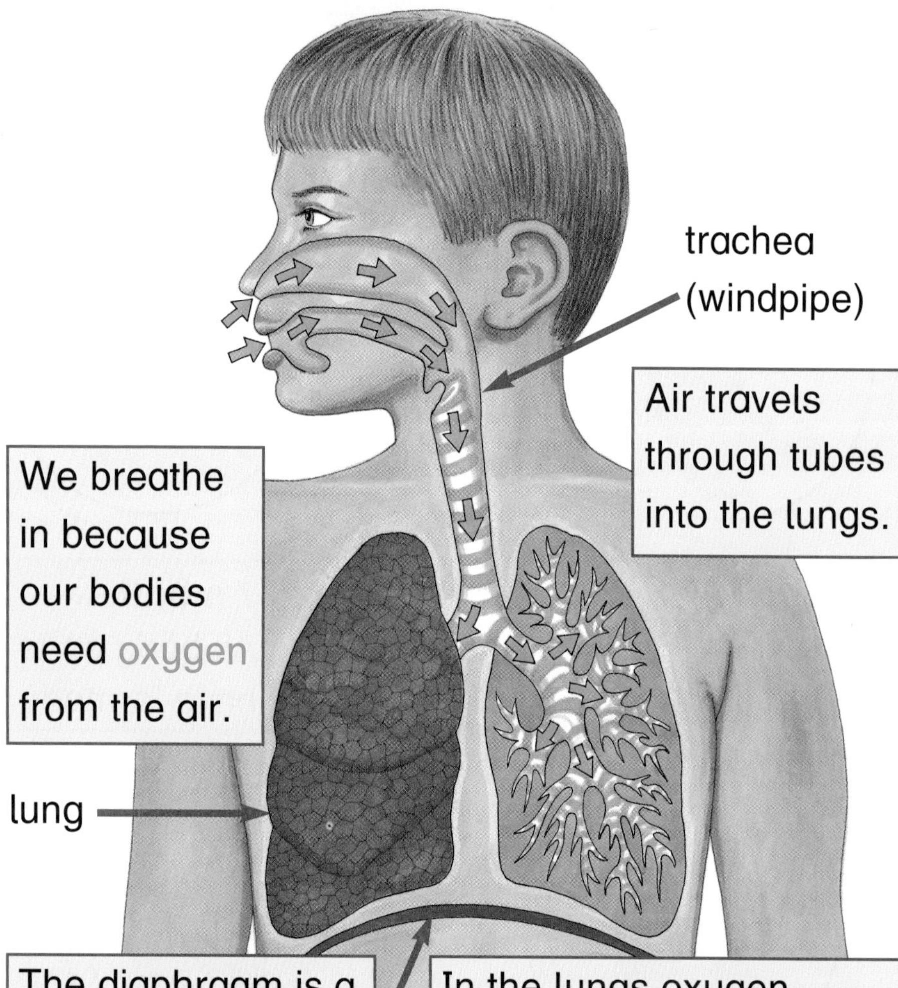

We breathe in because our bodies need oxygen from the air.

Air travels through tubes into the lungs.

The diaphragm is a sheet of muscle which pulls down, helping the lungs to fill with air.

In the lungs oxygen enters the blood system to be taken to the heart. Unwanted carbon dioxide leaves the blood ready to be breathed out.

Sneezing gets rid of particles like dust and smoke which irritate noses and lungs. Sneezes leave our mouths at about 160 kilometres per hour.

Sneezing can spread germs so it is always important to cover your nose and mouth with a handkerchief when you sneeze.

All about blood

Your heart is about the same size as your fist.

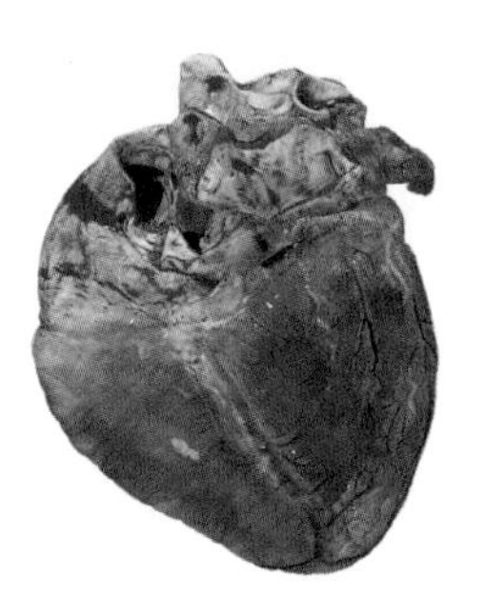

The heart pumps blood round the body so that every part receives oxygen and food. Arteries take blood from the heart. They branch into very tiny tubes called capillaries. These join up again to form veins. Veins take blood back to the heart.

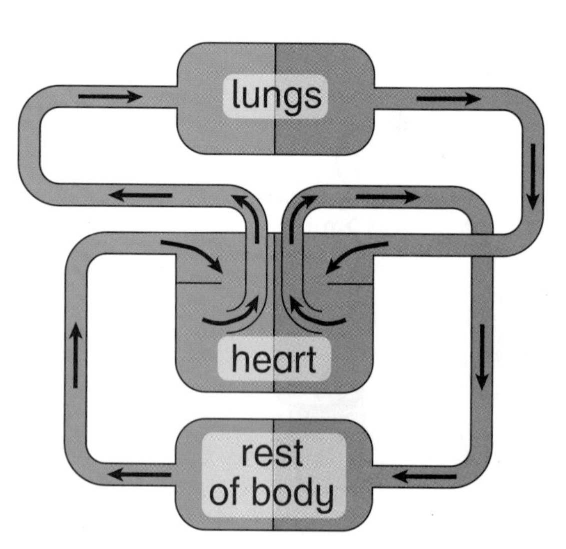

How blood travels round the body. This is called blood circulation.

What is in the blood?

Red blood cells carry oxygen. ➡

This is a white blood cell. White blood cells fight infection. ⬇

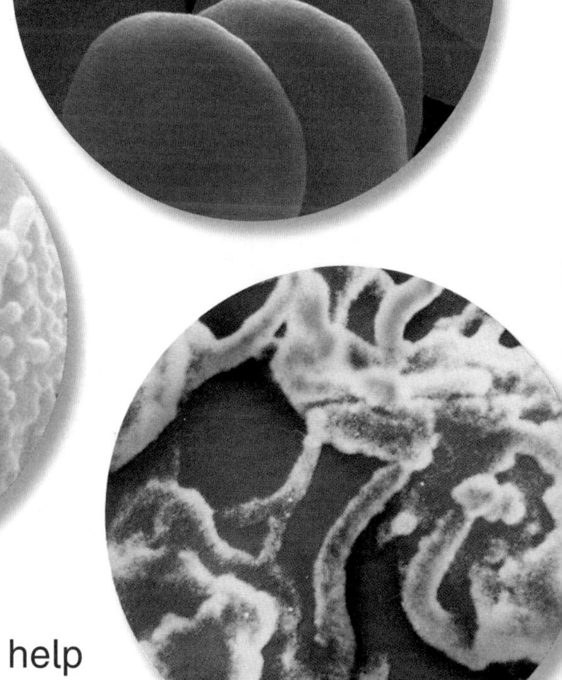

Platelets are tiny. They help to seal cuts and grazes. ➡

Red and white blood cells and platelets are in a clear liquid called plasma.

The food journey

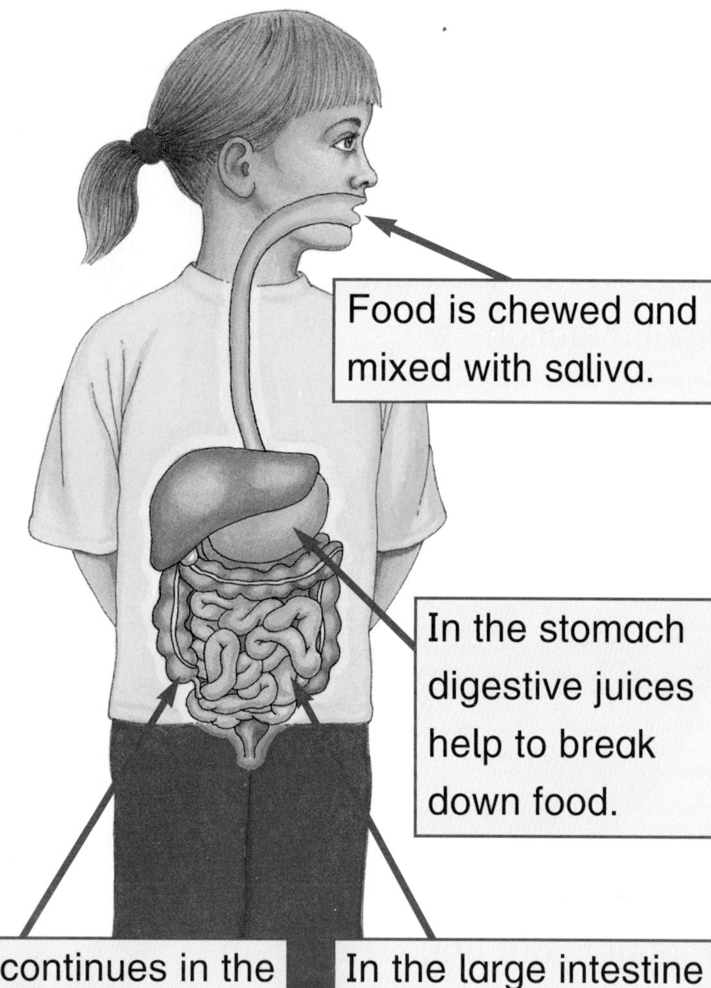

Digestion continues in the small intestine. Nutrients are collected by the blood and taken to the liver for processing.

In the large intestine water is absorbed. Waste is stored until it is passed out of the body.

Waterworks

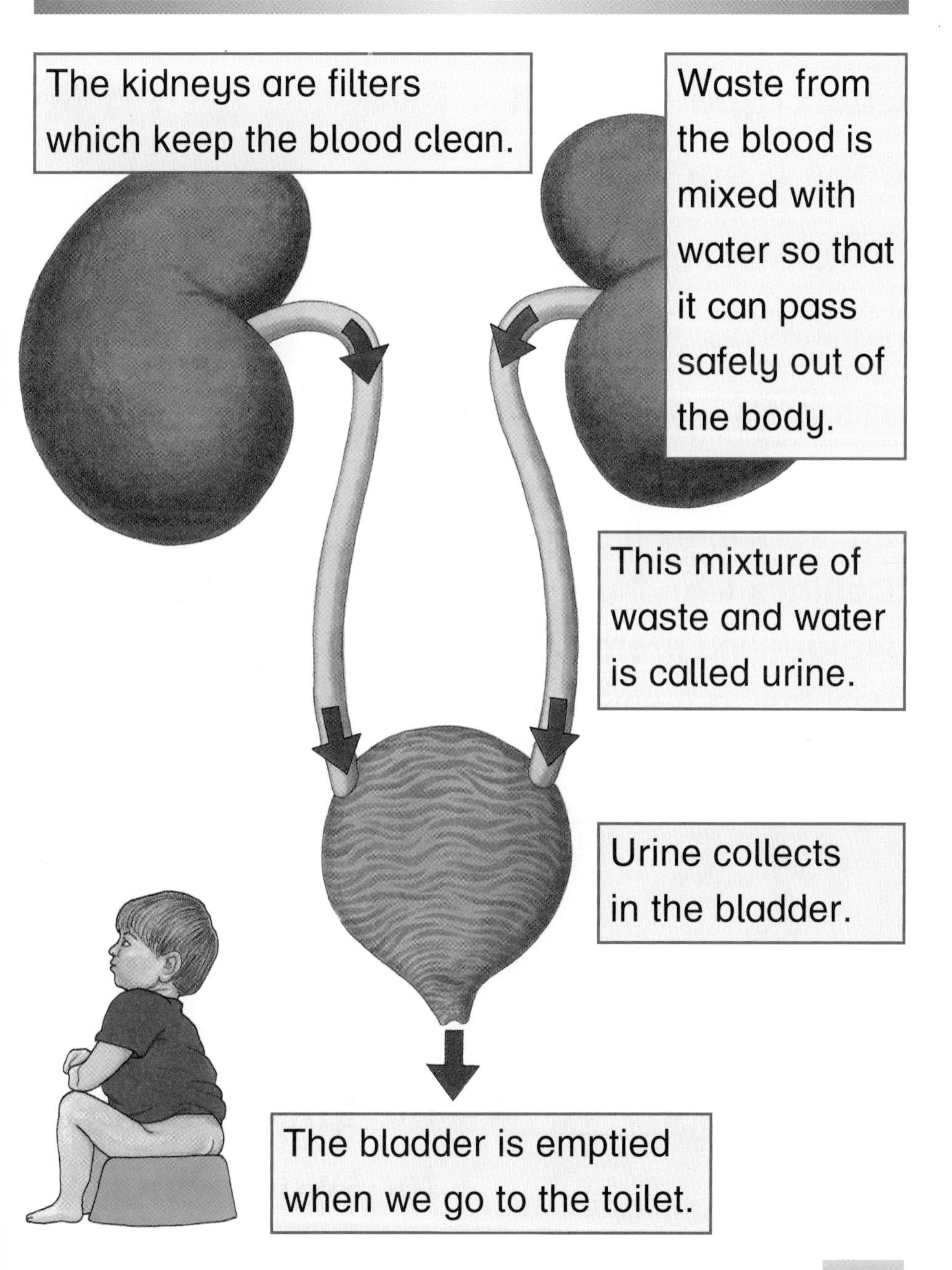
The kidneys are filters which keep the blood clean.
Waste from the blood is mixed with water so that it can pass safely out of the body.
This mixture of waste and water is called urine.
Urine collects in the bladder.
The bladder is emptied when we go to the toilet.

Check up on teeth

Each type of tooth does a special job.

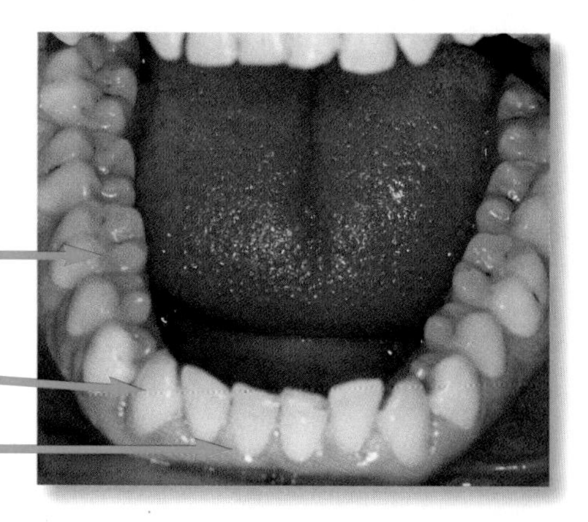

Incisors bite off chunks of food.
Canines tear chunks into smaller pieces.
Molars and **premolars** grind and chew pieces until they are small enough to swallow.

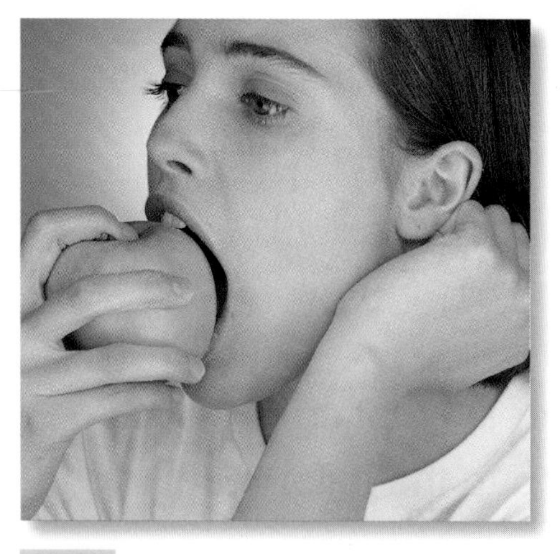

The pieces of food are mixed with saliva and moved around by the tongue ready for swallowing.

If food is left between teeth, bacteria can grow.

Bacteria produce acids which attack teeth. A cavity develops and the decay spreads.

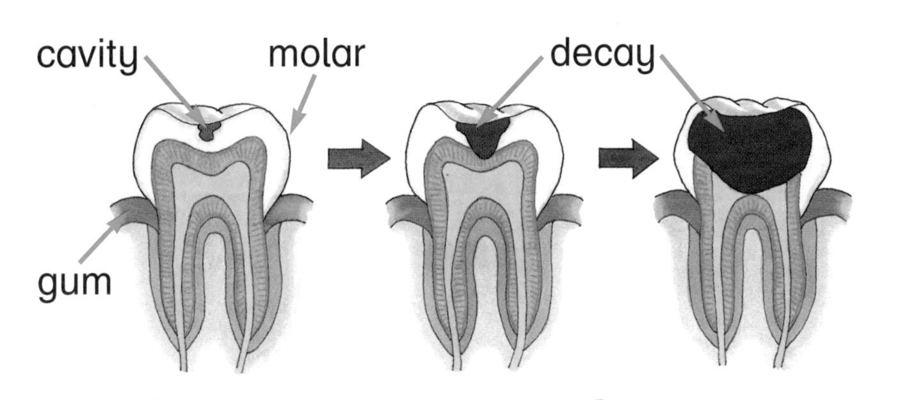

Caring for your teeth checklist

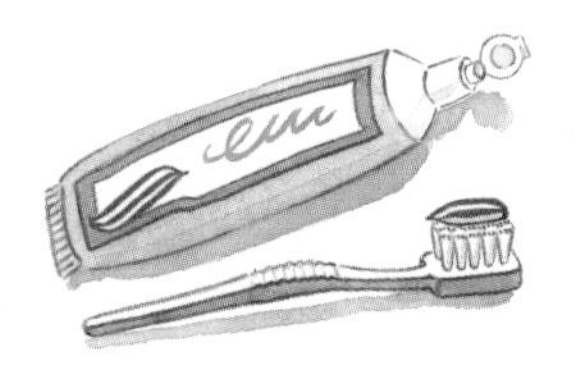

▲ Brush teeth thoroughly at least twice a day.

▲ Visit a dentist regularly.

▲ Avoid too many sugary foods and drinks.

Get to know your skeleton

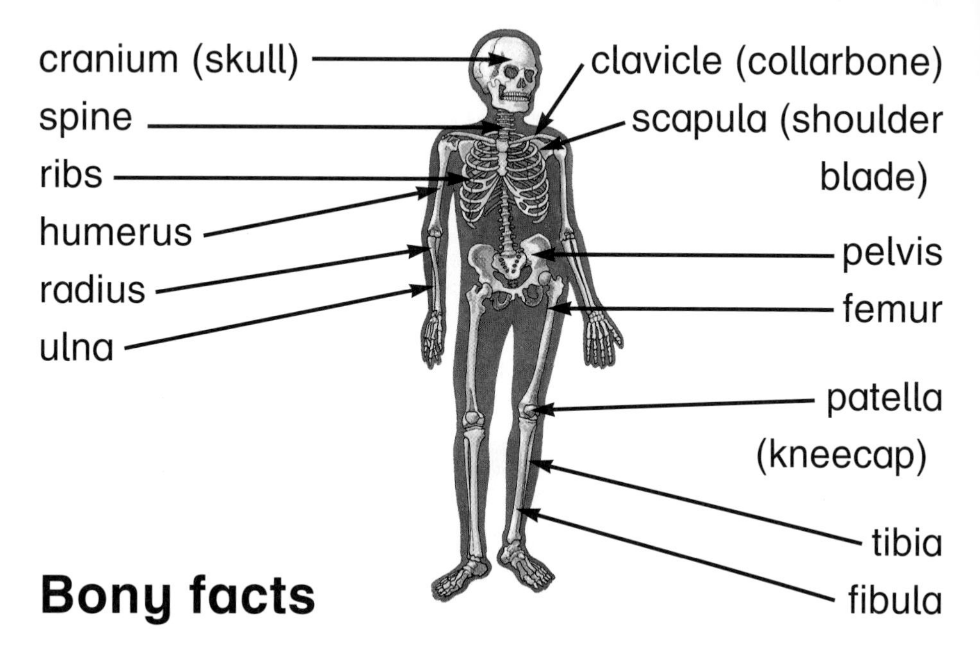

Bony facts

There are 206 bones in your body. Your bones keep growing until you are about 20 years old.

Why do we need bones?

- **They support the body.**
- **They protect soft body parts.**
- **They work with muscles to allow us to move.**

On the move

Every time you move, a joint is working. How many joints can you find in your body? Do they all move the same way?

Muscles usually work in pairs. They work by shortening.

To lift the arm the biceps muscle shortens.

To lower the arm the triceps muscle shortens.

The body's control centre

The brain is the control centre for our bodies. It is connected to every part of the body by a system of nerves.

The main route for nerves to the brain is inside the spine.

Different parts of the brain control different areas of the body.

speaking
moving
touching and feeling
hearing
seeing
balancing
thinking
remembering
tasting and smelling

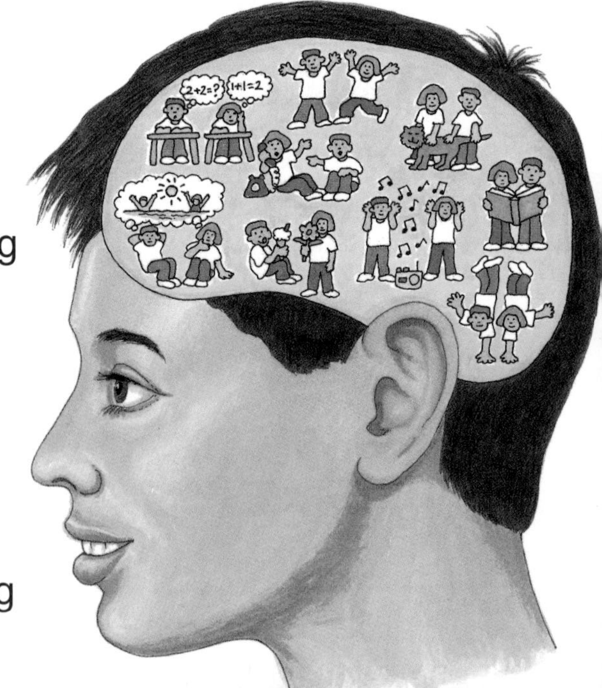

Feeling hot, feeling cold

Our bodies cannot work properly if they are too hot or too cold.

Warming up

Cooling down

How do we warm ourselves up when we feel cold?

How do we cool ourselves down when we feel hot?

Eye spy

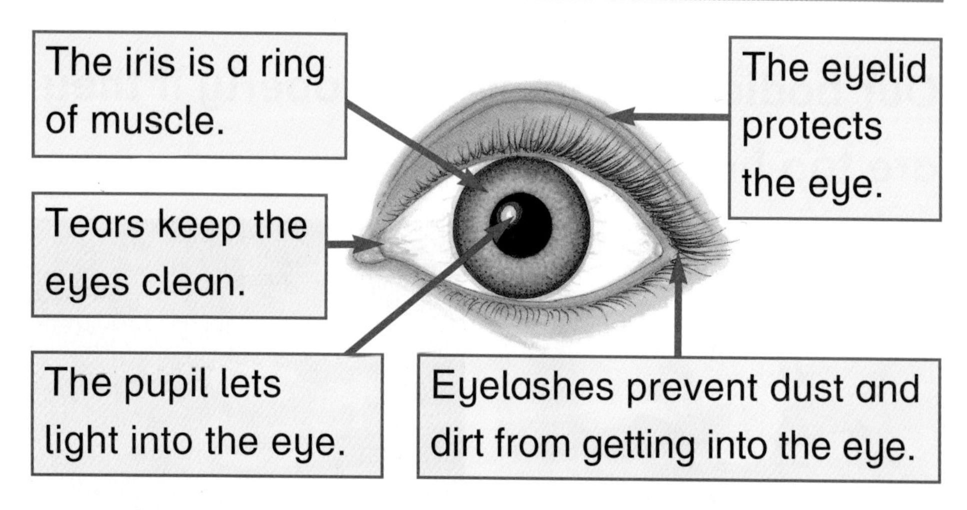

We see objects when light reflected from them enters our eyes. Nerves send messages to our brains and tell us what we see.

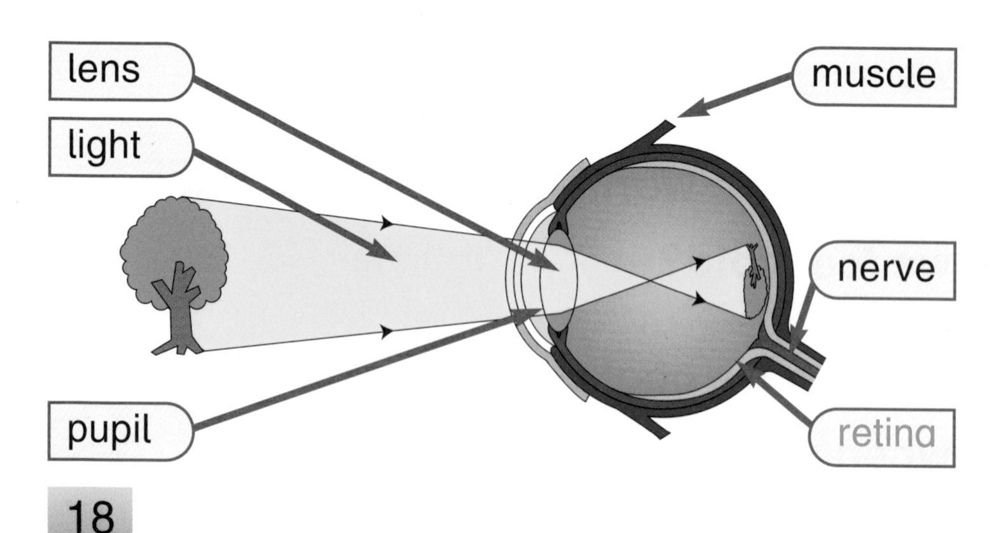

When it is dark our pupils are large. This lets more light in and helps us to see better.

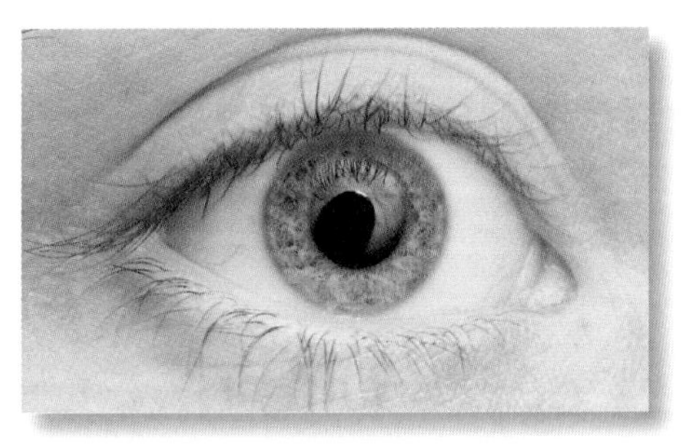

In the dark

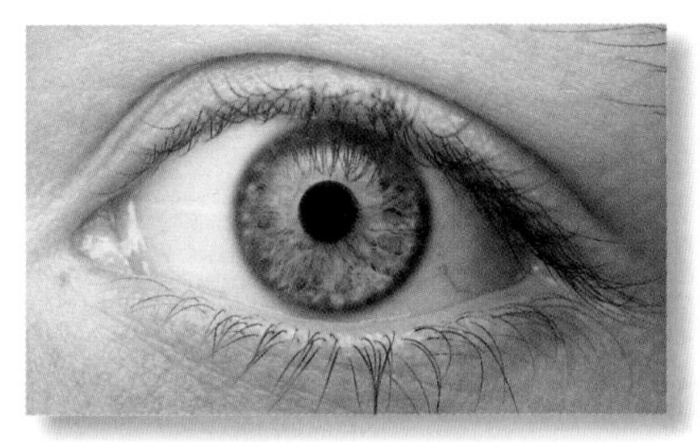

In the light

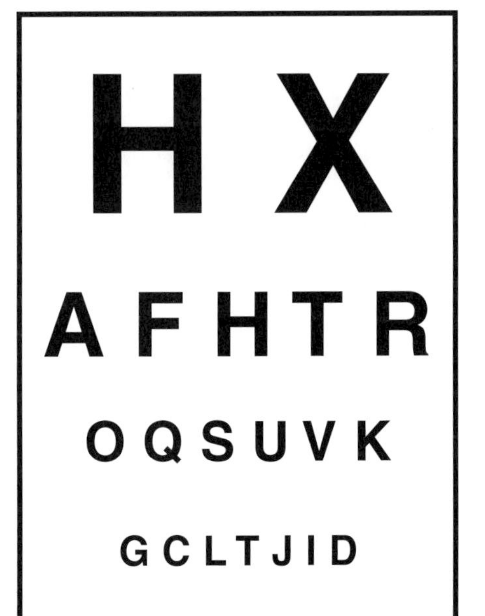

Some people wear glasses or contact lenses to improve their sight. Opticians use charts to test people's eyesight.

Feeling in touch

When we touch things we can feel whether they are hot, cold, soft, hard, sharp, smooth or rough. Nerves under the skin's surface send this information to the brain.

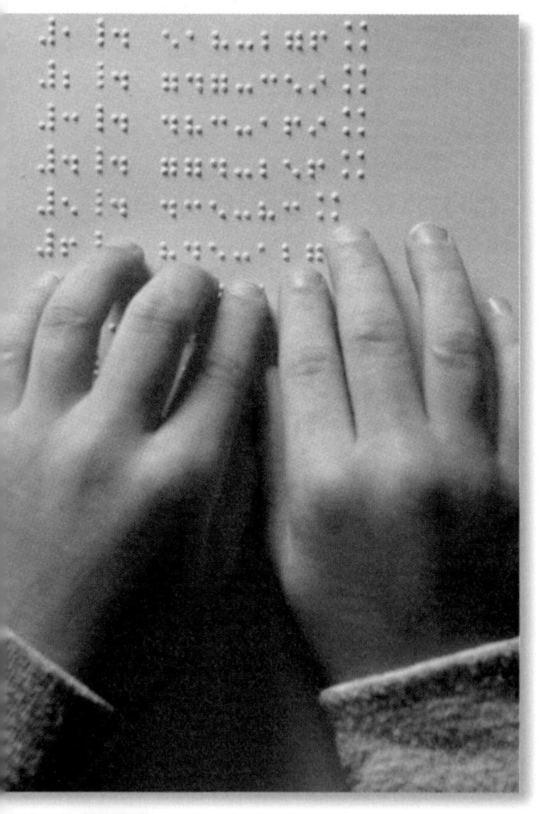

People who are blind can use the sense of touch to read. The Braille alphabet is made of raised dots which blind people feel with their fingers.

Smells good!

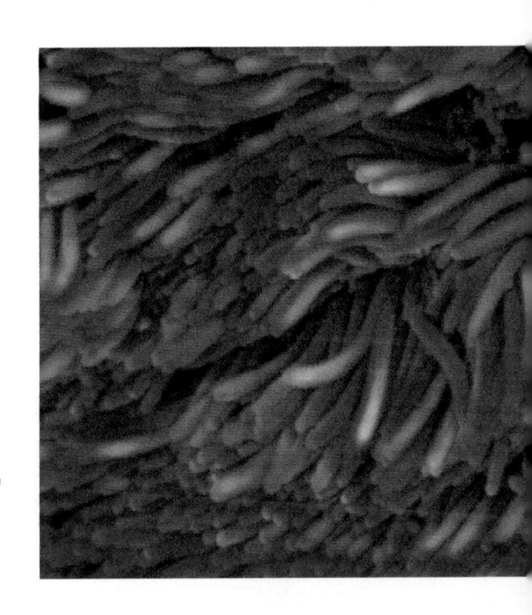

High up at the back of your nose are special cells.

These cells have 'hairs' which sense chemicals in the air we breathe.

Messages from these cells travel directly to the brain.

Smells are closely linked with memories. A familiar smell often reminds us of a place or event.

Tasty information

The tongue is covered with tiny bumps. There are about 10 000 taste buds amongst these bumps which help us to recognise what we are eating.

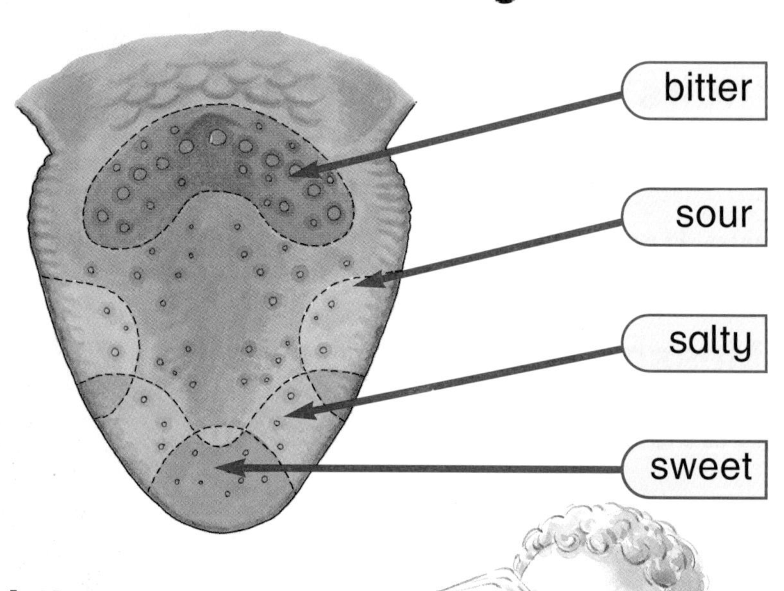

Try holding your nose closed whilst sampling foods. Can you taste the flavours?

Can you hear me?

Our ears are like very delicate scientific instruments which pick up the vibrations of sound.

Our ears are designed to collect sounds.

We can distinguish different kinds of sound.

We can pinpoint where sounds are coming from.

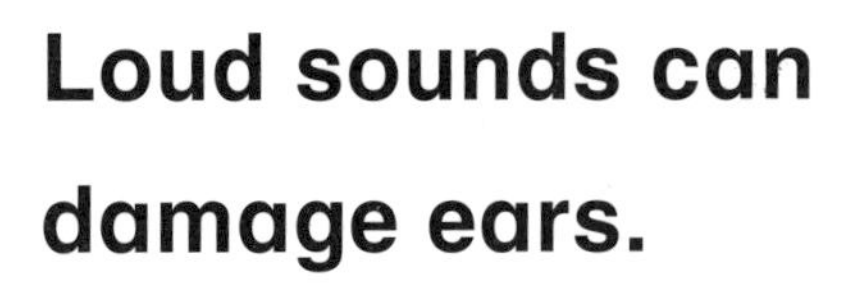

Loud sounds can damage ears.

Spot the senses

Look carefully at this picture. Find the things you could feel, taste, hear and smell.

Which things make you think about your sense of sight?

A healthy menu

A balanced diet helps to keep your body healthy. Choose food from each part of the menu chart and water to drink.

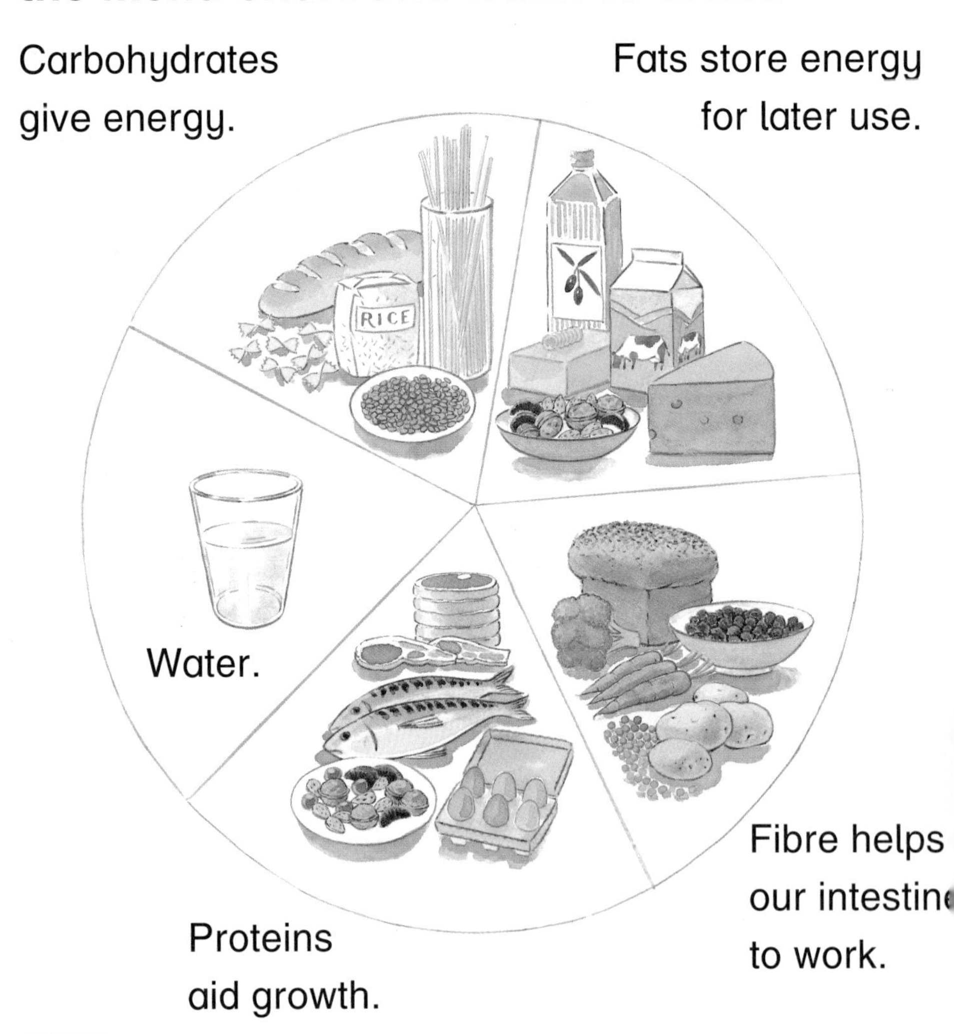

Foods contain vitamins which help you to stay healthy. These are some of the vitamins you need.

Vitamin A

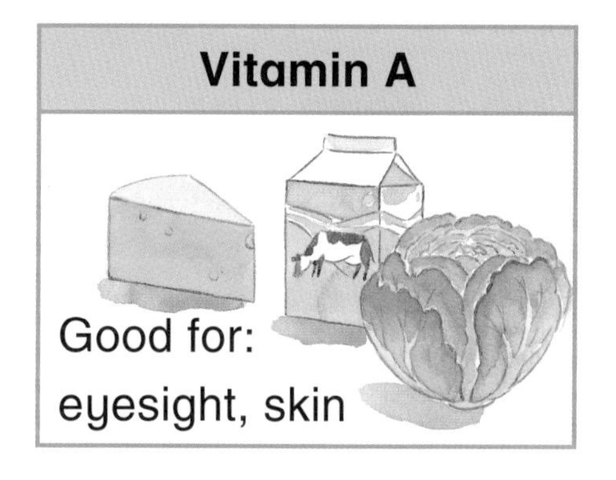

Good for:
eyesight, skin

Vitamin B

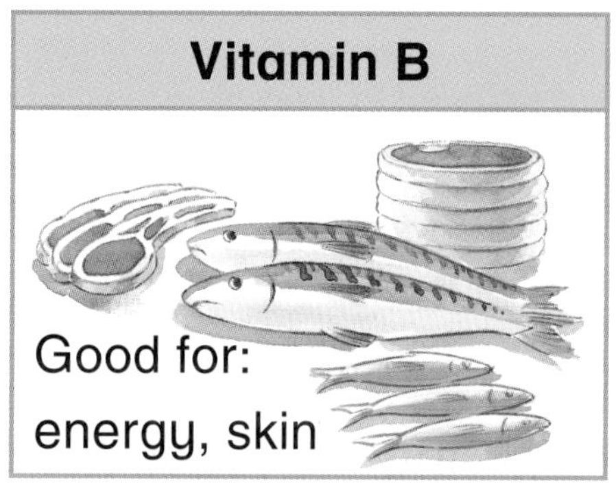

Good for:
energy, skin

Vitamin C

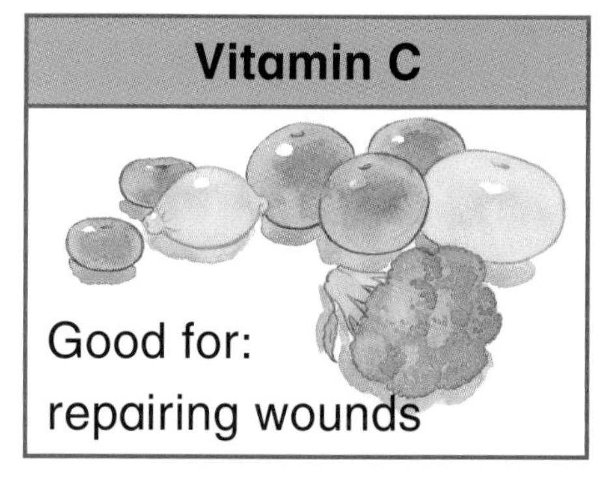

Good for:
repairing wounds

Vitamin D

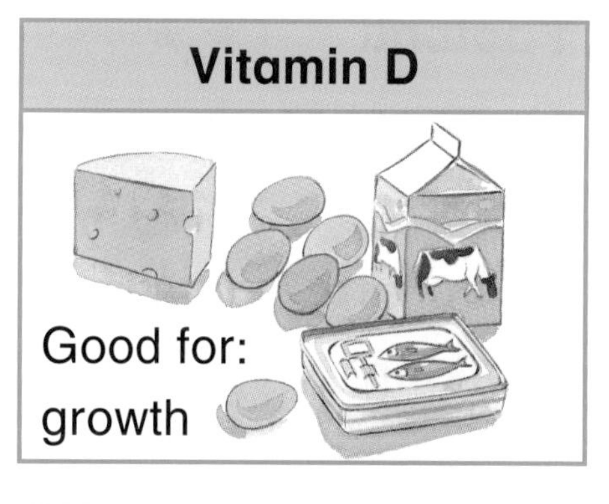

Good for:
growth

Vitamin E

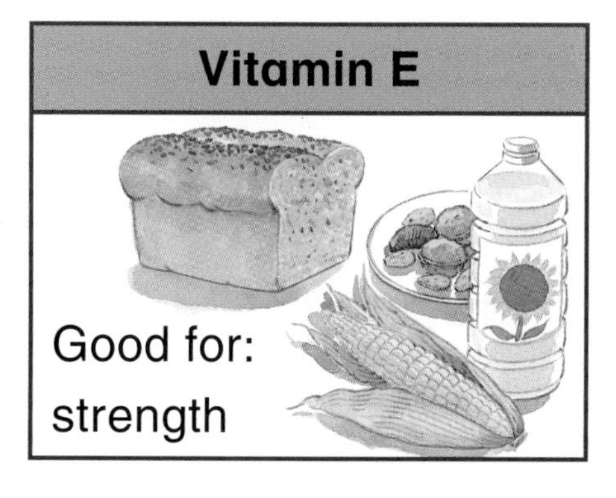

Good for:
strength

Vitamin K

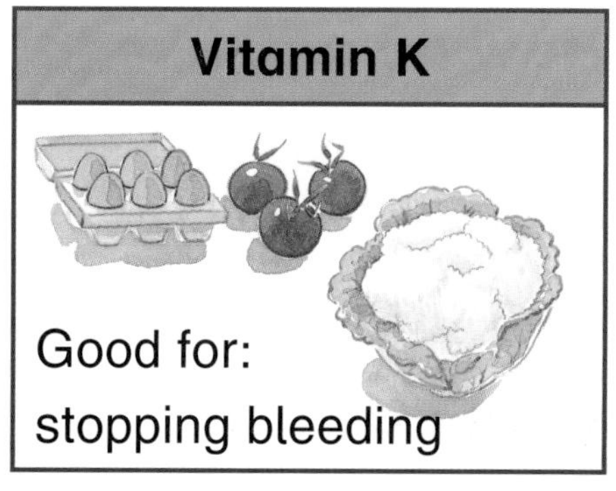

Good for:
stopping bleeding

Work, rest and play

There are many enjoyable ways to exercise. Exercise can help us to build strength and stamina and keep our bodies supple.

Exercise	Stamina	Strength	Suppleness
Cycling	★★★	★★	★
Football	★★	★★	★★
Gymnastics	★	★★	★★★
Jogging	★★★	★	★
Swimming	★★★	★★★	★★★
Walking	★		

How do you like to exercise?

Sleeping lets our bodies relax, repair and grow. We sleep for about one third of our lives!

What about drugs?

Medicines are special drugs which help our bodies to keep healthy or recover from illness.

It can be very dangerous to mis-use any drugs.

Think about each of these pictures.

When are drugs needed to keep us well?

When can drugs be dangerous?

Our amazing bodies

How can you tell which twin is which?

Check their thumb prints! Everyone's thumb print is different – even identical twins'.

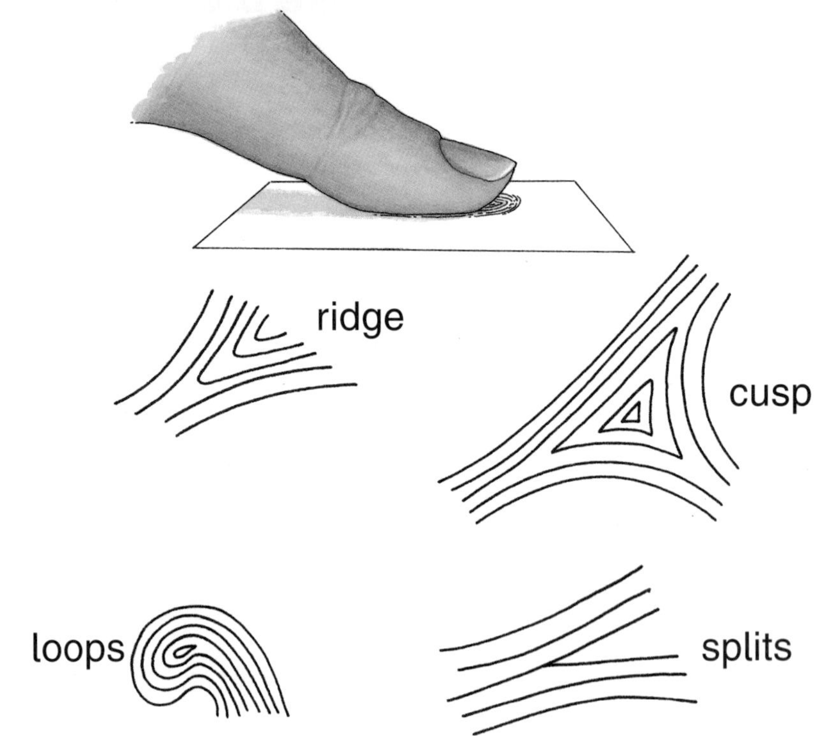

Glossary of words used in this book

bacteria *(p. 13)* microscopic (tiny) organisms (something living) each made of just one cell.

cavity *(p. 13)* a hole.

digestion *(p. 10)* the breakdown of food into chemicals the body can use.

germ *(p. 7)* a harmful organism.

nutrients *(p. 10)* the parts of food which our bodies need to keep healthy.

oxygen *(p. 6)* a gas which is part of air. All animals need to breathe in oxygen.

retina *(p. 18)* a screen at the back of the eye.

stamina *(p. 28)* the ability to keep going.

supple *(p. 28)* the ability to bend.

vitamins *(p. 27)* chemicals needed by the body.

womb *(p. 4)* the special place in a woman's body where a baby grows.

Index

arteries 8

bladder 11
blood 8–9, 10, 11
bones 14
brain 16, 18, 20, 21

carbon dioxide 6

diaphragm 6
digestion 10
drugs 29

ears 23
eyes 18–19

germs 7

heart 4, 5, 6, 8

intestines 10

joints 15

kidneys 11

liver 10
lungs 6, 7, 8

muscles 3, 6, 14, 15, 18

nerves 4, 16, 18, 20
nose 7, 21, 22

oxygen 6, 8, 9

saliva 10, 12
skin 2
stomach 4, 10

teeth 12–13
tongue 22

veins 8
vitamins 27

windpipe 6
womb 4